POLICE HORSES

HORSES THAT PROTECT

Loren
Spiotta-DiMare

Enslow Elementary

The **Horses That Help** *series is dedicated to my sister, Sheryl, and niece, Katherine. We are so lucky to have each other and horses in our lives. I'd also like to extend a special thank you to Rozin Smith for contributing so many beautiful photographs to the series. —Loren Spiotta-DiMare*

American Humane Association™

The nation's voice for the protection of children & animals™

Since 1877, American Humane Association has been at the forefront of virtually every major advance in protecting children, pets, and farm animals from cruelty, abuse, and neglect. Today we're also leading the way in understanding the human-animal bond and its role in therapy, medicine, and society. American Humane Association reaches millions of people every day through groundbreaking research, education, training, and services that span a wide network of organizations, agencies, and businesses. You can help make a difference, too. Visit www.americanhumane.org today, call 1-866-242-1877, or write to American Humane Association at 1400 16th Street NW, Suite 360, Washington, DC 20036.

Enslow Elementary, an imprint of Enslow Publishers, Inc. Enslow Elementary® is a registered trademark of Enslow Publishers, Inc.

Copyright © 2014 by Loren Spiotta-DiMare

Library of Congress Cataloging-in-Publication Data

Spiotta-DiMare, Loren.
    Police horses : horses that protect / Loren Spiotta-DiMare.
      pages cm. — (Horses that help with the American Humane Association)
    Includes bibliographical references and index.
    Summary: "Opens with a true story about a police officer and his horse and follows with the history of police horses, what breeds are used, the training involved, what the horses do on the job, and what happens to police horses when they retire"— Provided by publisher.
    Audience: Ages 8-up.
    Audience: Grades 4 to 6
    ISBN 978-0-7660-4218-6
    1. Police horses—Juvenile literature. 2. Horses—Training—Juvenile literature. I. Title.
    HV7957.S66 2014
    363.2—dc23
                         2012051303

Future editions:
Paperback ISBN: 978-1-4644-0379-8
EPUB ISBN: 978-1-4645-1209-4
Single-User PDF ISBN: 978-1-4646-1209-1
Multi-User PDF ISBN: 978-0-7660-5841-5

Printed in the United States of America

102013 Lake Book Manufacturing, Inc., Melrose Park, IL

10 9 8 7 6 5 4 3 2 1

Photo Credits: AP Images/The Oregonian, Thomas Boyd, p. 39; Courtesy of Officer Luis Camacho, p. 9; Courtesy of EasyCare Inc., p. 15; Jorg Hackemann/Shutterstock.com, p. 1; © William Johnston/iStockphoto.com, p. 32; © 2009, Martin Kavanagh, pp. 1, 4, 8, 14, 27, 28; Stuart Monk/Shutterstock.com, pp. 19, 35; The Museum of the City of New York/Art Resource, NY, p. 13; Shutterstock.com, pp. 1 (horse head clipart), 3; © Rozina Smith, pp. 21, 30, 37, 38; © Craig Sotres, pp. 5, 12, 16, 22, 26, 34, 41; © Vicki Wright Photos, p. 24; © Jerilyn Weber, pp. 10, 25, 42, 44.

Cover Photo: © 2009, Martin Kavanagh (Lieutenant Bob Marelli on Chief); Shutterstock.com (horse head clipart).

CONTENTS

Lieutenant Bob Marelli has loved horses from an early age. It was a great honor when he became the head of the Newark Mounted Police.

Lieutenant Bob Marelli and Lieu: A True Story

Officer Henry Marelli and his two sons were policemen in Newark, New Jersey. Newark is a large and very busy city. The younger son, Bob, shared his father's love of horses and started riding when he was five years old. "My dad had been a Marine," he says. "He put me in the saddle and said, 'Sit straight or you are getting off.'" From that moment on, Lieutenant (Lt.) Bob Marelli became devoted to horses and discipline, doing things the proper way, which would be very important during his career as a police officer.

Lt. Marelli joined the police force when he was twenty-one. At first, he worked in the patrol car and motorcycle units. Later, he was asked to join the mounted police. These officers ride on horseback. Over time, he reached the rank of lieutenant and became the head of the department.

Police horses have many jobs, but their two most important responsibilities are street patrol and crowd control. When they are on street patrol, officers ride their horses up and down the city streets, keeping an eye out for any crimes. When they are on crowd control, usually during special events when many people gather together, the mounted police are there to make sure no fights break out and everyone stays safe. Dangerous situations can happen at any time, so police horses must be smart, well trained, and brave. It is also important for an officer and his horse to work well together as a team.

At one time, there were eighteen horses in the Newark mounted unit. Lt. Marelli was responsible for choosing and training them. In 2000, he needed a horse for himself. Then, a six-year-old Thoroughbred joined the force. He was bay, a dark brown, with a white blaze on his face and white on three of his lower legs. Lt. Marelli named him Lieutenant and called him Lieu ("Loo") for short.

Lieu was a high-spirited young horse. Lt. Marelli started training him in the indoor ring to practice the different gaits, the speeds that a horse moves in. Horses walk, trot, and canter on a lunge line, which looks like a long dog leash. Trotting is almost like human jogging. Cantering is faster than trotting but slower than galloping. In time, Lt. Marelli began riding Lieu so he would understand commands given from the officer's legs and the reins, which connected to two bits in Lieu's mouth. A bit is a tiny bar that sits between the horse's upper and lower teeth. Lt. Marelli's officers used two bits for extra control.

Police horses have to get used to busy city streets. They must learn to not be afraid of crowds and loud noises.

Next, they worked in the outside ring and then went out on the streets so Lieu would get used to the sights and sounds of the city. He was jumpy at first. Everything caught his attention. So they started out slowly, first walking up and down a quiet street. Then, they walked a half a block and next around a full block. After about six months, Lieu settled down and understood his job.

For the next eleven years, Lt. Marelli and Lieu patrolled the streets of Newark. During Special Details, patrols that are out of the ordinary and require all the horses, Lieu was always the point horse, or head horse, leading in front of the others. He knew his position and liked it.

Lt. Marelli and Lieu were also involved in many dangerous situations. Once, they were called to help out during a house fire. After the fire trucks arrive, it is the mounted police officer's duty to control traffic, shut down the street, and keep people away from the fire. Lieu was frightened by the flames but stood still as he had been trained. Another time, during a festival when the crowd

FAST FACT

Police horses wear badges. They are considered law enforcement officers.

Lt. Marelli and Lieu retired from the Newark police force together in 2010. The strong emotional bond they shared as partners continues.

went out of control, a chair was thrown and hit Lieu in the neck. Again, he stayed calm. He always seemed to understand he had to be good to keep Lt. Marelli safe and allow him to do his job.

The two formed a very close bond. When Lt. Marelli retired from the police force in 2010, after forty years of service, Lieu retired with him. "I love that horse," the lieutenant says. "He is like a son to me."

Chapter 1

The History of Police Horses

The idea of protecting people while on horseback developed in England more than three hundred years ago. Instead of police departments, sheriffs and their deputies watched over citizens in towns and cities. When the British began to move to America in the 1600s, mounted law enforcement continued here. In those days, towns, cities, and farms could be very far apart, so patrolling on horseback was an excellent way to keep colonists safe.

In 1845, one of the first police departments formed in New York City. Just a year later, a mounted unit was created to help control horseback riders, carriages, and wagons that were traveling at fast speeds and causing accidents in the busy city. The unit was very helpful in lowering the number of horse-related accidents.

Police horses can now be found in cities as well as state, county, and national parks throughout the country. These mounted units continue a proud tradition and

This postcard shows the mounted police of New York City in 1905.

A police horse must look as professional as the uniformed officer on his back. Notice the polished hooves.

must look professional at all times. Officers wear police uniforms, and the horses are well groomed. Their tack (saddles, blankets, and bridles) are always kept clean and in good condition. Some units pick horses that have dark-colored coats. Others place borium, a rough metal, on the horses' shoes to keep them from slipping on the streets. And some units polish their horses' hooves so the horses look their best from head to hoof.

FAST FACT

Some police horses wear boots, which are like tennis shoes for horses, to protect their feet and help them walk without slipping.

Chapter 2

Police Horse Breeds

Police horses must be smart, brave, calm, and dependable. It is in a horse's nature to take off at the first sign of danger. But police horses should not spook, or jump, spin, or run off if something frightening happens. For example, if an ambulance passes by, the horse should not react. This is especially important on city streets because a runaway horse can easily crash into a car or building, injuring his officer and himself.

A police officer and her horse patrol the busy streets of New York City. As a well-trained police horse, he stays calm as traffic zooms by behind him.

The size of a police horse is also important. A horse's height is measured in hands from the withers to the hooves. The withers are located between the shoulders. A hand is equal to four inches. Riding horses usually are between fourteen and a half and sixteen and a half hands (fifty-eight and sixty-six inches). Mounted units usually prefer horses that are at least sixteen hands (sixty-four inches tall). A tall horse gives the officer a better view of his or her surroundings.

FAST FACT

Before there were rulers and tape measures, people had to find other ways to measure things. To measure the height of a horse, a man would hold his hand sideways, then stack one hand on top of the other all the way to the withers. Later, the hand came to equal four inches.

Tall mounts allow police officers to take a better look at what is going on in a crowd.

Many breeds of horses can be trained as police horses, but a few are especially good at the job. These include draft horse crosses, quarter horses, standardbreds, and Thoroughbreds.

Draft Horse Crosses

Draft horses are large, heavy breeds originally used for farmwork, such as plowing. They are known as "gentle giants" because they can be eighteen hands (seventy-two inches) or taller. They are friendly, calm, and happy to work with people. Some popular draft breeds are Clydesdales, Percherons, and Belgians. If a horse is a draft cross, it means one parent is a draft breed and the other parent is a lighter breed, such as a quarter horse or Thoroughbred. These crosses are very popular police horses because they are gentle, do not scare easily, and are a little smaller than draft horses, making them easier to ride.

This police horse is a Clydesdale cross. Notice his large, thick build and shaggy legs. These traits are from the horse's Clydesdale parent.

The author's horse, Elwood, is a sorrel quarter horse.

FAST FACT

They are called quarter horses because in colonial times, these horses were raced for a quarter of a mile on village streets.

Quarter Horses

Quarter horses, originally ridden by cowboys while herding cows, stand between fourteen and sixteen hands (fifty-six and sixty-four inches). They are found in all colors. Sorrel, a reddish brown, is the most common. They are smart, willing, people-friendly, and calm.

Standardbreds

Standardbreds are usually harness racing horses. They pull a small carriage, called a sulky, with a driver. These horses stand between fifteen and sixteen hands (sixty and sixty-four inches). The most common colors are bay and brown. They are very smart, and according to Suzanne D'Ambrose, a former police officer and law enforcement instructor, "Because they are used to noises at racetracks, they get used to mounted patrol training easily. The breed is also known to have good feet. Even though police horses will wear shoes since they will patrol the streets, having strong hooves is important."

Law enforcement instructor Suzanne D'Ambrose rides Indy, a standardbred.

Thoroughbreds

Thoroughbreds are tall, sleek, and lean. They are bred for speed. Many Thoroughbreds race with jockeys on their backs, while others compete in different equine sports, such as jumping. They are usually fifteen and a half to seventeen hands (sixty-two to sixty-eight inches). Most Thoroughbreds are brown, bay, chestnut, black, or gray.

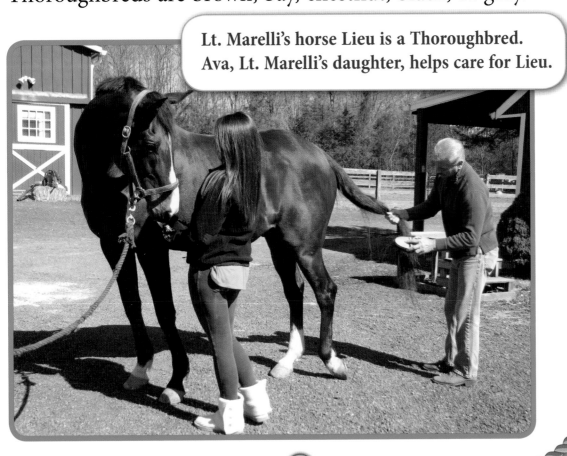

Lt. Marelli's horse Lieu is a Thoroughbred. Ava, Lt. Marelli's daughter, helps care for Lieu.

Chapter 3

Police Horses on the Job

People often think of horses as large dogs, but these two animals see the world in very different ways. Dogs are predators, animals that hunt; horses are prey, animals that are hunted. Although a dog would probably attack if threatened, a horse's first reaction is to run away. So to be able to train police horses to ignore traffic, trains, sirens, and other loud city noises that would normally scare them is truly amazing.

Aside from remaining calm at all times, police horses must also be physically fit because they will be working long hours. They must also be able to work alone. This can be especially difficult for horses because they are herd animals and like being in a group.

Lt. Bob Marelli (left) and Officer Luis Camacho stand with Chief, a standardbred. People love to interact with the police horses. Petting the animals helps people relax, making it easier for them to talk to the officers.

When Lt. Bob Marelli was supervisor of the mounted unit, he had many responsibilities. He chose and trained the horses, trained his officers, and assigned posts, which are the areas the mounted officers patrol. He had to make sure the horses were properly fed and cared for by a farrier, a person who shoes a horse, and a veterinarian. He also went on patrol himself.

Lt. Marelli (left) rides Chief while Officer Camacho is on Judge, also a standardbred. They patrol the streets of Newark.

Officer Luis Camacho worked with Lt. Marelli and has been a mounted officer for more than thirteen years. "I love the job," he says. "It is a different kind of policing. People are always happy to see us. They approach to pet the horses and talk with us. Some even give us information to help solve crimes."

Officer Camacho's devotion to police horses is easy to see. He has fallen off his horse twice in his career, which can happen in the line of duty. Once when he was hurt, his first thought was to hold on to his horse so the horse would not run away and possibly get hit by a car. While still on the ground, waiting for help to arrive, he held on to his horse's reins. He really did not have to. His horse stood still and nuzzled the officer's face, as if to say, "Do not worry, I will not leave you." As partners, a police officer and his or her horse depend on each other to keep safe.

Sergeant Michael Puccetti and Roadblock, a Clydesdale cross, protect the Morris County Park system in New Jersey.

Not all police horses work in cities. The Morris County Park system in New Jersey has a mounted unit with four horses: a Thoroughbred, a Clydesdale cross, and two quarter horses. Roadblock, the Clydesdale cross, stands seventeen and a half hands (seventy inches). He is a favorite mount of Sergeant (Sgt.) Michael Puccetti, who runs the unit. Roadblock was purchased from a farm in Canada that trains horses for police work. He is a large, handsome horse that knows his job well.

FAST FACT

Depending on which part of the country the police horses work in, a big part of their job is to help their officers search for missing children, elderly, and injured people. They also assist in searching for evidence, escaped prisoners, and criminals who are on the run.

Police horses must stand still and remain calm while children stroke them.

Like Lt. Marelli, Sgt. Puccetti grew up riding horses. He has been a police officer for more than twenty-five years. Morris County has the largest park system in the state. Mounted officers patrol all the grounds, perform search and rescue when needed, participate in parades, and are called out for special events, such as the Fourth of July fireworks. During the holidays, they patrol shopping malls. They are also asked to give presentations at schools.

Sgt. Puccetti agrees with Officer Camacho by saying horses are wonderful at making people feel comfortable and safe. "People are more likely to approach an officer on a horse than on foot or in a car," Sgt. Puccetti explains.

Police horses need to stand patiently when people approach. Because children often run up to the horses to pet them, the horses must be friendly and accept the attention without biting or kicking. They must also be careful not to step on little feet.

Chapter 4

Training Police Horses

Mounted police officers have many duties. They ride through the streets to keep them safe, issue parking tickets, stop people committing crimes, lead parades, and control crowds during special events, such as festivals or concerts, and disturbances, such as riots. Police horses must learn to push through crowds of people if necessary and not panic. They must be under control at all times, especially in dangerous situations.

Officers from the New York City Police Department Mounted Unit march in the famous St. Patrick's Day Parade, March 17, 2012. Police horses are used to large crowds and loud noises.

Some horses are given to police departments. Others are bought. Horses with the best potential, the ability to do something well, are accepted. Sgt. Puccetti has a checklist to fill out when looking at a horse. Some of the questions on the list include: When was the horse last ridden? Is he quiet to work around and under saddle? Is he spooked by anything? Does he load into a trailer well?

Has he ever been in a parade? Is he afraid of water? If the horse passes the checklist, he is brought to the mounted unit's stable for a one-month trial period.

A large part of police horse training is getting the horses used to strange sights and sounds. Many exercises are performed in a riding ring. For example, the horses will be asked to walk over a tarp (a plastic covering), weave around flares, pass by color balloons, or push a big ball. Horses would avoid these objects on their own, so they must learn to trust that their officers will not lead them into danger. The lessons begin at a good distance, and slowly the officer asks his horse to move closer to the object. "If a horse does not wish to go closer, I simply talk to him in a soft voice and remain where he is most comfortable," law enforcement instructor Suzanne D'Ambrose says. "If he takes one step closer, I praise as if he just won a gold medal."

Sgt. Puccetti demonstrates how Roadblock can walk over a blue tarp without being scared. The horse has learned to trust that Sgt. Puccetti will keep him safe.

Police horses must also learn to ignore traffic sounds, trains, firecrackers, and other loud noises. Suzanne plays a CD of all kinds of sounds while the horses in training are eating or being groomed. At first, the sounds are played at a distance. Horns may be honked or a firecracker shot off. Eventually, the horse is brought closer to the sound until he remains calm and ignores it. City police horses are ridden in a parking lot next, then one quiet block, and finally busier streets.

Training a police horse to be completely reliable can last a few weeks to a year. Every horse is different and learns at his own pace. The process cannot be rushed. "It takes as long as it takes," Lt. Bob Marelli says. "The horses let us know when they are ready."

Officers must also be trained. Most mounted units require at least one year of police experience. Mounted training usually takes six to ten weeks.

Roadblock, the Clydesdale cross, walks in between two flares. Normally, horses run away from fire, but police horses are trained to follow orders.

This police horse in training playfully nuzzles a police officer. They will build a strong, trusting relationship as they learn to work together.

Officers training to be mounted police must like horses, but they do not need to have riding experience. In fact, Sgt. Puccetti prefers that they do not have riding experience so he does not have to fix bad habits. They can learn the proper way to ride right from the start.

The officers are first taught to feed and groom their horses, including cleaning their hooves. Then, they spend every day learning how to ride in a ring. When they can stay balanced in the saddle without slipping off, they start to ride outside the ring. When they become good, confident riders, they begin more difficult challenges, such as learning to ride through smoke, near fires, and through tunnels. These early days of training help police officers form a bond with their horses and become a strong working team.

Chapter 5

When Police Horses Retire

Police horses often spend many years on the job. But there will come a time when they get too old or too tired to keep working full-time and should retire. Some are sent to special retirement farms to live with other horses in small herds. There are special rescues that accept donations to take care of retired police horses and other retired working horses. They depend on money from kind people to help them.

Lieu enjoys his retirement from the Newark police force in a stable near Lt. Marelli's home. Lt. Marelli's daughter, Ava, also loves spending time with Lieu.

Other former police horses that are still fit enough to be ridden may be adopted by families. They usually make excellent trail horses because they have always been around different sights and sounds.

Rich had not ridden in many years, so when he bought a new home with a barn on the property, he wanted to buy a safe and well-trained horse. He found Patrone, a retired police horse. Rich had always ridden quarter horses, which are usually fifteen to sixteen hands (sixty to sixty-four inches). Compared to the horses Rich was used to, Patrone, a black Percheron cross, was huge at eighteen hands (seventy-two inches). "He was magnificent," Rich says. "Very powerful but also calm, easygoing, and well mannered."

When Lt. Bob Marelli retired from the Newark Police Department, his horse, Lieu, was eighteen years old and able to retire too. Because the two had such a special relationship, Lt. Marelli decided to adopt Lieu himself.

He was able to find a wonderful stable near his home to keep Lieu. Lieu is very happy there. He enjoys spending his days grazing with his pasture pals or trail riding with Lt. Marelli.

Lt. Marelli's daughter, Ava, shares her dad's love of horses and also rides Lieu. Lt. Marelli tries to go riding a few times a week. But even if he does not have time, he still visits Lieu every day.

Because horses can live well into their twenties or early thirties, Lt. Marelli and Lieu can look forward to riding through the countryside together for many years to come.

Glossary

borium—A rough material put on a horse's shoe to keep it from slipping on slick surfaces.

canter—The gait of a horse that is faster than a trot but slower than a gallop.

discipline—Training to do things the proper way.

gait—One of several speeds a horse moves in, such as a walk, trot, and canter.

potential—The ability to do something well.

tack—Horse equipment, such as saddles, blankets, and bridles.

trot—The gait of a horse that is similar to human jogging. The front leg and opposite back leg move forward at the same time.

withers—The tallest point on a horse's back; it is between the shoulders.

Learn More

Books

Andrekson, Judy. *Brigadier: Gentle Hero.* Toronto: Tundra Books, 2009.

Apte, Sunita. *Police Horses.* New York: Bearport Pub. Co., 2007.

Mezzanotte, Jim. *Police (Working Animals).* New York: Benchmark Books, 2010.

Nagle, Jeanne. *Working Horses.* New York: Gareth Stevens Pub., 2011.

Internet Addresses

American Humane Association
 <http://www.americanhumane.org>

HorseChannel.com
 <http://www.horsechannel.com>

Index